URUGUAY

DISCOVERING
SOUTH AMERICA
History, Politics, and Culture

URUGUAY

Charles J. Shields

Mason Crest
Philadelphia

Mason Crest
450 Parkway Drive, Suite D
Broomall, PA 19008
www.masoncrest.com

Printed and bound in the United States of America.

CPSIA Compliance Information: Batch #DSA2015.
For further information, contact Mason Crest at 1-866-MCP-Book.

First printing
1 3 5 7 9 8 6 4 2

Library of Congress Cataloging-in-Publication Data
        on file at the Library of Congress

        ISBN: 978-1-4222-3305-4 (hc)
        ISBN: 978-1-4222-8648-7 (ebook)

Discovering South America: History, Politics, and Culture series ISBN: 978-1-4222-3293-4

DISCOVERING SOUTH AMERICA: History, Politics, and Culture

Argentina	Chile	Guyana	Suriname	South America:
Bolivia	Colombia	Paraguay	Uruguay	Facts & Figures
Brazil	Ecuador	Peru	Venezuela	

Table of Contents

KEY ICONS TO LOOK FOR:

Words to Understand: These words with their easy-to-understand definitions will increase the reader's understanding of the text, while building vocabulary skills.

Sidebars: This boxed material within the main text allows readers to build knowledge, gain insights, explore possibilities, and broaden their perspectives by weaving together additional information to provide realistic and holistic perspectives.

Research Projects: Readers are pointed toward areas of further inquiry connected to each chapter. Suggestions are provided for projects that encourage deeper research and analysis.

Text-Dependent Questions: These questions send the reader back to the text for more careful attention to the evidence presented there.

Series Glossary of Key Terms: This back-of-the book glossary contains terminology used throughout this series. Words found here increase the reader's ability to read and comprehend higher-level books and articles in this field.

Discovering South America

James D. Henderson

SOUTH AMERICA is a cornucopia of natural resources, a treasure house of ecological variety. It is also a continent of striking human diversity and geographic extremes. Yet in spite of that, most South Americans share a set of cultural similarities. Most of the continent's inhabitants are properly termed "Latin" Americans. This means that they speak a Romance language (one closely related to Latin), particularly Spanish or Portuguese. It means, too, that most practice Roman Catholicism and share the Mediterranean cultural patterns brought by the Spanish and Portuguese who settled the continent over five centuries ago.

Still, it is never hard to spot departures from these cultural norms. Bolivia, Peru, and Ecuador, for example, have significant Indian populations who speak their own languages and follow their own customs. In Paraguay the main Indian language, Guaraní, is accepted as official along with Spanish. Nor are all South Americans Catholics. Today Protestantism is making steady gains, while in Brazil many citizens practice African religions right along with Catholicism and Protestantism.

South America is a lightly populated continent, having just 6 percent of the world's people. It is also the world's most tropical continent, for a larger percentage of its land falls between the tropics of Cancer and Capricorn than is the case with any other continent. The world's driest desert is there, the Atacama in northern Chile, where no one has ever seen a drop of rain fall. And the world's wettest place is there too, the Chocó region of Colombia, along that country's border with Panama. There it rains almost every day. South America also has some of the world's highest mountains, the Andes,

Vacationers enjoy an afternoon on the beach in Punta del Este.

and its greatest river, the Amazon.

So welcome to South America! Through this colorfully illustrated series of books you will travel through 12 countries, from giant Brazil to small Suriname. On your way you will learn about the geography, the history, the economy, and the people of each one. Geared to the needs of teachers and students, each volume contains book and web sources for further study, a chronology, project and report ideas, and even recipes of tasty and easy-to-prepare dishes popular in the countries studied. Each volume describes the country's national holidays and the cities and towns where they are held. And each book is indexed.

You are embarking on a voyage of discovery that will take you to lands not so far away, but as interesting and exotic as any in the world.

(Opposite) Penguins wade into the surf at Punta del Este. Oil pollution along the coast of Uruguay is an environmental problem that kills hundreds of penguins each year. (Right) Montevideo, the capital of Uruguay, is known for its beaches, including fashionable Playa Pocitos, which is rimmed by high-rise buildings.

1 Land of Green Rolling Plains

URUGUAY, THE SMALLEST Spanish-speaking nation in South America, is about the size of the state of Washington. The Río Uruguay forms its western border with Argentina. Brazil lies to the north and east. The Atlantic Ocean and the Río de la Plata, an *estuary* of the Atlantic, border Uruguay in the south. Most of Uruguay is a green rolling plain, interrupted at two points by highlands of low hilly ridges. The narrow Atlantic coastal plain is sandy and marshy, occasionally broken by shallow lagoons.

Two Land Regions

Uruguay can be divided into two major land regions: the coastal plains and the interior lowlands.

The coastal plains curve along the Río Uruguay, the Río de la Plata, and the Atlantic Ocean. They cover about one-fifth of Uruguay. But most of the nation's population is concentrated in this region, especially along the southern coast. Montevideo, the largest city in Uruguay and its capital, lies on the coast near the point where the Río de la Plata and the Atlantic meet. Small family farms and large plantations occupy much of the western and southwestern coastal plains, which have Uruguay's richest and deepest soil. Beaches, sand dunes, and lagoons line the Atlantic shore.

The interior lowlands cover about 80 percent of Uruguay. Vast, grass-covered plains and hills and numerous rivers and streams make this area an ideal place for raising livestock. Sprawling ranches occupy most of the region, and small cities and towns dot the countryside. The Río Negro, the largest river in the interior, flows southwestward through the heart of the lowlands. A dam on the river forms Uruguay's only large lake, Lago Rincón del Bonete.

A long, narrow chain of highlands curves across the interior from the Brazilian border almost to the southern coast. Uruguayans call these high-

Words to Understand in this Chapter

estuary—a water passage where the ocean tide meets a river current.
migratory—traveling seasonally to another place.
pampero—a strong, cold wind from the west or southwest that sweeps across the Argentine pampas.
reservoir—a human-made body of water used to conserve resources or create power.
temperate—in a warm, comfortable temperature range.
tributary—a stream or river flowing into a larger body of water.
water table—the upper limit of the ground soaked with underground water.

lands Cuchilla Grande (Big Knife) because knifelike formations of rock jut through the soil on many of the ridges. Overall, though, these hilly areas are remarkably featureless. The highest point in Uruguay, Cerro Catedral, rises 1,683 feet (514 meters) in the Cuchilla Grande.

A Water-Rich Land

Uruguay enjoys an abundance of water. Experts believe that in the language of the country's original inhabitants, "Uruguay" means "rivers of fishes." Large bodies of water bound Uruguay on the east, south, and west. Even the boundary with Brazil consists mostly of small rivers. Lakes and lagoons are numerous, and a high *water table* makes digging wells easy.

A gaucho, or cowboy, guides a herd of cattle through green pastureland. Uruguay's low-lying grasslands are ideal for cattle ranching.

Three systems of rivers drain the land. Rivers flow westward to the Río Uruguay, eastward to the Atlantic and the tidal lagoons bordering the ocean, and south to the Río de la Plata. The longest and most important of the rivers draining westward is the Río Negro, which crosses the entire country from northeast to west before emptying into the Río Uruguay. But the Río Uruguay, which marks the border with Argentina, has low banks. During heavy rains, the river overflows, causing disastrous floods over enormous areas. A dam on the Río Negro at Paso de los Toros helps control the flow into the Río Uruguay. Behind the dam is a huge *reservoir*—Lago Rincón del Bonete. This reservoir is the largest artificial lake in South America. Flowing into the Río Negro is the Río Yi, its main *tributary*.

Cars ride down a street covered by ocean foam during a heavy winter windstorm. High winds can be a problem in Uruguay, particularly in the winter when the *pampero* blows from Argentina. (Because of its location in the Southern Hemisphere, seasons in Uruguay are the opposite of those in the United States.)

Quick Facts: The Geography of Uruguay

Location: Southern South America, bordering the South Atlantic Ocean, between Argentina and Brazil

Area: (slightly smaller than the state of Washington)
- **total:** 68,065 square miles (176,220 sq km)
- **land:** 67,061 square miles (173,620 sq km)
- **water:** 1,004 square miles (2,600 sq km)

Borders: Argentina, 360 miles (579 km); Brazil, 612 miles (985 km)

Climate: temperate, with damp springs and winters

Terrain: mostly rolling plains and low hills; fertile coastal lowland

Elevation extremes:
- **lowest point:** Atlantic Ocean—0 feet
- **highest point:** Cerro Catedral—1,683 feet (514 meters)

Natural hazards: seasonally high winds (the *pampero* is a chilly and occasional violent wind that blows north from the Argentine pampas), droughts, floods; with so few mountains to act as weather barriers, all locations are particularly vulnerable to rapid changes in weather fronts

Source: CIA World Factbook 2015.

The rivers flowing east to the Atlantic are generally shallower, but their water level rises and falls more frequently. Many empty into lagoons in the coastal plain. The largest coastal lagoon, Laguna Merín (Lagoa Mirim in Brazil), forms part of the border with Brazil. A half-dozen smaller lagoons, some freshwater and some saltwater, line the coast farther south.

A Mild Climate

Uruguay lies in a *temperate* zone. It is the only Latin American country completely outside the Tropics. The climate is mild and generally the same through the country. Northwestern Uruguay, however, is farther from large bodies of water and therefore has warmer summers and milder and drier winters than the rest of the country.

In most of Uruguay, spring is usually damp, cool, and windy; summers are warm; autumns are mild; and winters are chilly and uncomfortably damp. High humidity, high winds, and fog are common. Winter warm spells can be abruptly broken by a strong *pampero*, a chilly and occasionally violent wind from the Argentine pampas (plains). There are no mountains to stop the wind's rush across the land. However, pleasant summer winds off the ocean can moderate warm daytime temperatures.

Rain falls evenly throughout the year. Amounts increase from southeast to northwest. Montevideo receives 37 inches (94 centimeters) annually, and the city of Artigas receives about 50 inches (127 cm) per year. As in most temperate climates, rain is the product of passing cold fronts. Thunderstorms occur frequently in the summer.

Environmentally Sensitive Wetlands

Much of Uruguay consists of rolling plains that are used for grazing sheep and cattle. But Uruguay's wetlands are special for a number of reasons.

Located on the Atlantic coast of Uruguay, the eastern wetlands contain fragile ecosystems. Butía palms, found nowhere else, grow in dense groves covering thousands of acres. Fields of tall grasses, floating grasses, rushes, and reeds support traditional Uruguayan crafts, especially basket weaving. Among the area's animals are a number of threatened or endangered species, such as the field deer, river wolf, straw cat, mountain lion, and dragon duck. River otters and carpinchos (large, semiaquatic rodents) roam the wetlands, too. More than 147 bird species, including many aquatic birds, breed here. Some live in the wetlands year-round; others are *migratory*. The warm, shallow waters are good places for fishing boats to find yellow clams, mussels, and shrimp.

Human activity has stressed the wetlands ecosystems. Hilly areas are used to raise livestock. Other parts of the wetlands have been converted to rice fields; rice farmers' dikes, ditches, and dams cut off the water flow, and their pesticides and fertilizers kill off insects. Tourism has spurred new highway construction, along with increased water pollution and soil breakdown. In the face of these pressures, the government of Uruguay is working with international agencies to find ways to protect its natural resources.

TEXT-DEPENDENT QUESTIONS
1. What are the two major land regions of Uruguay?
2. What is the highest point in Uruguay?
3. How much rain falls in Montevideo annually?

(Opposite) A cobbled street passes beneath an arched gateway in the city walls of Novo Colônia do Sacramento. This colonial settlement on the coast of Uruguay was established in 1680 by Portuguese adventurers from Brazil. (Right) Uruguay's president, Luis Batlle Berres, and his wife meet Argentina's Juan and Eva Perón on a boat in the middle of the Río de la Plata, 1948.

2 A Forward-Looking Nation

URUGUAY WAS A part of Spain's colonial empire in the Americas until the early 1800s. Then revolutionary forces drove out the Spanish. Brazil laid claim to Uruguayan territory until a peace treaty established Uruguay as an independent nation in 1828.

Throughout most of its history, Uruguay has enjoyed a democratic form of government, although bitter party rivalries caused much bloodshed in the 1800s and a *guerrilla* movement in the 1970s led to a harsh crackdown that resulted in more than a decade of military dictatorship. Democracy was restored in the 1980s. In 2001 and 2002, the financial troubles of its neighbors, Brazil and Argentina, harmed Uruguay's economy, which has recovered slowly.

Early Settlement and Independence

Long before the arrival of European explorers in Uruguay, the Charrúa Indians hunted in the wetlands. They defended their territory fiercely. When the Spanish explorer Juan Díaz de Solís approached them by boat in 1516, they killed him and most of his men as soon as the Europeans landed on the riverbank. For the rest of the 16th century, the Charrúa turned away all outsiders. By the 17th century, though, the natives had begun trading with the Spanish.

For the next few centuries, the Portuguese and the Spanish competed to control trade on the Atlantic coast of South America. In 1680 the Portuguese built the settlement of Colônia do Sacramento (present-day Colonia, Uruguay) beside the Río de la Plata. A century earlier, on the opposite bank,

Words to Understand in this Chapter

amnesty—pardon granted to a large group of individuals by the government.
annex—to incorporate territory (often seized by force) into a nation.
buffer state—a neutral state lying between two larger powers that are rivals of each other.
gauchos—South American cowboys.
guerrilla—a person who battles a government or military using unconventional means such as sabotage.
urban—relating to the city.
viceroyalty—an often large overseas territory governed on behalf of a monarch by an appointed official called a viceroy.
villa—a country estate or home belonging to a wealthy person, or a suburban residence resembling such a home.

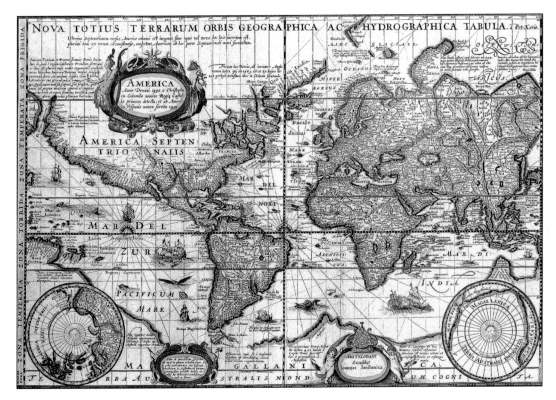

The vertical line through the continent of South America on this 17th-century map marks the boundary established by the 1494 Treaty of Tordesillas. Spain was granted the land west of the line; Portugal, the land to the east. Uruguay held a key strategic position between Spanish Argentina and Portuguese Brazil.

the Spanish had permanently established Buenos Aires. In 1726, to counteract the threat of Portuguese expansion in the Banda Oriental area (the lands east of the Río Uruguay), the Spanish built a fort south of Colônia at Montevideo.

This statue of José Gervasio Artigas stands in Montevideo's Independence Plaza. He is one of Uruguay's national heroes.

In 1776 this region was joined administratively with the territory of present-day Argentina in the Spanish *viceroyalty* of La Plata. Buenos Aires became the viceroyalty's major political and economic center, though it had some competition from Montevideo. Outside these coastal cities, *gauchos* (cowboys) herded cattle on the sparsely populated and virtually lawless plains.

In 1810 upper-class citizens of Buenos Aires rebelled against colonial rule, setting in motion the movement for independence that would eventually free all of Spain's South American possessions. The following year Uruguayan gaucho José Gervasio Artigas led a revolt against the Spanish at Montevideo. After several years of successes and setbacks, Artigas won control of the Banda Oriental. But the Portuguese in Brazil saw an opportunity to expand their territory. They overwhelmed the Uruguayans and in 1817 *annexed* the land.

Escaping to Paraguay, Artigas inspired those who would be later dubbed the "33 Immortals"—33 patriots who, under the leadership of Juan Antonio Lavalleja and with the support of Argentine allies, finally liberated Uruguay from Brazil in 1828. A peace treaty established Uruguay as an independent *buffer state* between Argentina and Brazil.

The Colorados Versus the Blancos

During the 19th century, two warring political parties split the loyalties of Uruguayans. The liberal Colorados wore red hatbands to distinguish themselves from the conservative Blancos, who wore white. Civil war broke out often as the two sides fought for control of the country, which opened the door to intervention from Uruguay's powerful neighbors, Brazil and Argentina. But when Paraguay entered the conflict by aligning itself with the Blancos, the Colorados united with Brazil and Argentina to fight against Paraguay in the War of the Triple Alliance (1865–1870). Although the Colorados and their allies won the war, both sides suffered heavy losses. Bitter fighting continued between the two rival parties until 1872, when they finally agreed to share leadership of Uruguay by alternating presidents.

Despite the conflicts, Uruguay prospered, thanks in large part to the involvement of Great Britain. British immigrants and investors introduced new wool, meat, and railroad industries. They also replaced poor-quality Spanish cattle with their own higher-quality breed. By the end of the 19th century, Uruguay had become a key supplier of beef, leather, and wool to the Western world. Immigrants from Europe, especially Italy, arrived by the tens of thousands looking for farmland and work.

In the early part of the 20th century, the Colorados elected José Batlle y Ordóñez to the presidency. He served two terms, from 1903 to 1907, and from 1911 to 1915. An unusually far-sighted leader, Batlle launched social programs that included medical and retirement plans, free education, laws protecting workers' rights, and public health reforms. But wealthy landowners blocked his attempts for fairer land-distribution policies.

During World War I in 1917, Uruguay broke off relations with Germany. Also that year, its constitution was amended to separate the church and the state. In 1920, when the victors of World War I formed the League of Nations—an international organization similar in some ways to the United Nations—Uruguay immediately joined.

Successes and Setbacks

Uruguayan democracy faced a setback in 1931 when the Blancos elected President Gabriel Terra, who demanded broader powers for the government. To stifle threats of revolt, Terra established a mild dictatorship with the help of his party. When the Colorado Party returned to power in 1938, a new constitution was adopted that reversed Terra's policies and strengthened individual liberties. During World War II, Uruguay sided with the Allied cause and cut off relations with Germany, Italy, and Japan. It joined the United Nations when that organization was established in 1945.

During the 1960s, corruption in government eroded the country's prosperity. In 1967 an *urban* guerrilla movement, the Tupamaros, initiated a campaign of terroristic violence to overthrow the government. Four years later, the military took control of the government, dissolved Uruguay's congress, and hunted down Tupamaros as well as peaceful political opponents.

The military controlled Uruguay's political affairs until 1984, when Julio María Sanguinetti won the presidential election. Most Uruguayans were relieved when his government restored some democratic traditions and offered *amnesty* to political enemies. But there were no new policies established to help repair Uruguay's damaged economy.

In 1990 Luis Alberto Lacalle took office. Lacalle's plans to cut back on wages and reduce the government budget were necessary but unpopular. In 1994 Sanguinetti won a new term as president, serving until 1999. For his second term Sanguinetti expanded Uruguay's international trade.

Uruguay experienced political tension in the first years of the 21st century. Economic emergencies in Argentina and Brazil, as well as an outbreak of hoof-and-mouth disease among cattle, crippled Uruguay's economy. Jorge Batlle Ibáñez, president from 1999 to 2005, spent much of his term attempting to reverse the crisis. His successor, Tabaré Vásquez, inherited a healing but still fragile economy. During Vásquez's presidency, Uruguay enjoyed strong economic growth and the percentage of people living in poverty dropped sharply. Vásquez left office in 2010, but was re-elected president in November 2014.

During his first term as president, Tabaré Vásquez focused on reducing poverty and maintaining economic stability. He left office in 2010, but was reelected to a second term in 2014.

TEXT-DEPENDENT QUESTIONS

1. What Amerindian tribe hunted in Uruguay before the arrival of Europeans?
2. Who was the Uruguayan gaucho that led a revolt against the Spanish in 1811?
3. What urban guerrilla group tried to overthrow the government in the 1960s?

(Opposite) The state-owned La Teja oil refinery in Montevideo. Because Uruguay has no petroleum reserves, it must import all the oil it needs; as a result, the country's fuel prices are among the highest in Latin America. (Right) Fresh fruit is available at the Barrio Reus market. Agriculture is an important part of Uruguay's economy.

3 "The Switzerland of South America"

IN COMPARISON WITH many Latin American countries, Uruguay is fairly prosperous. The World Bank, an international development-assistance organization, estimated Uruguay's 2014 gross domestic product (GDP) per capita at $20,500. This placed Uruguay solidly within the ranks of middle-income nations worldwide. (GDP per capita, which measures each citizen's average share of a nation's annual economic activity, is similar to per capita income.)

A Livestock-Based Economy

The foundation of Uruguay's economy is four centuries old. In 1603, Spanish colonists released cattle and horses on the open plains of what is now Uruguay. The livestock thrived in the mild climate and vast natural pasturelands. By the early 1700s, there were millions of cattle in the region.

Cattle raising, which had begun almost by accident, provided Uruguay with highly profitable exports—animal hides and finished leather. (Until refrigeration, meat itself could not be transported great distances.)

But over the next 150 years, the most rapid population growth happened in Montevideo, not the countryside. Prosperity attracted waves of job-seeking immigrants from the urban centers of Italy and Spain. Farm workers from Uruguay's *rural* areas migrated to Montevideo and other towns, drawn by the hope of better wages. Small industries, many owned by foreigners, needed workers to process the great quantity of agricultural goods arriving from the ranches and farms. Montevideo's workshops began turning out footwear, clothing, wine, tobacco, paper, and furniture.

"The Switzerland of South America"

By the early 20th century, Uruguay had achieved enough growth to earn the nickname "the Switzerland of South America." Livestock exports—mainly beef, mutton, and wool—and handmade goods noted for their craftsmanship created a high standard of living. Ambitious social welfare programs

Words to Understand in this Chapter

rural—relating to the countryside.
textiles—goods made with natural fibers.
Third World—term used to describe the poorest nations of the world; "developing nations" is synonymous.

Uruguay is one of the leading meat producers in the world.

spread wealth throughout the society. In the first two decades of the 20th century, President José Batlle y Ordóñez launched radical social programs to improve education, labor conditions, and public health. Uruguay's middle class grew, and the country gained a reputation for social harmony.

But when export earnings dropped drastically during the Great Depression of the 1930s, Uruguay was hit hard. The government was forced to slash its social programs, and poverty became common, though not so widespread as in *Third World* countries.

The second half of the twentieth century reestablished Uruguay as a stable, middle-income country. But by 2000, economic troubles in Argentina and Brazil—two of Uruguay's important business partners—took a toll as the two nations sharply reduced trade and investment in Uruguay. In 2002, unemployment rose to 20 percent and banking activity was briefly suspended, leading to widespread riots.

The economy soon recovered, however. Uruguay's GDP grew by 8 percent a year, on average, between 2004 and 2008. This enabled the country to repay more than $1 billion of its foreign debt in 2006. A global financial crisis in 2009 has slowed Uruguay's economic growth, but did not stop it altogether.

Uruguay's large, well-educated middle class has been a key to its social stability. Extreme poverty remains uncommon. Almost all Uruguayan families own a radio and television set. Uruguay has about two dozen daily newspapers. The largest are *El País* and *El Día* in Montevideo. Uruguay's constitution guarantees freedom of the press.

Good roads link all parts of Uruguay, but the country's railroad system, which is owned and operated by the government, is old and undependable. Most Uruguayans rely on the government-run bus system to go between cities and towns. A number of private companies also offer bus service.

Greatest Resource

Uruguay's most valuable natural resource is still its land. The country's grasslands provide excellent natural pasture for livestock. Uruguay's leading manufacturers process beef, hides, and wool. Montevideo serves as Uruguay's major ocean port.

Most of Uruguay's businesses and industries are privately owned, though the national government controls most utilities, much of the

Quick Facts: The Economy of Uruguay

Gross domestic product (GDP*):
$69.78 billion.

GDP per capita: $20,500.

Natural resources: arable land, hydropower, minor minerals, fish.

Agriculture (7.5% of GDP): soybeans, rice, wheat; beef, dairy products; fish; lumber, cellulose.

Industry (20.4% of GDP): food processing, electrical machinery, transportation equipment, petroleum products, textiles, chemicals, beverages.

Services (72.1% of GDP): finance, transportation, communication, schools, hospitals, government agencies, tourism.

Inflation: 8.8%

Foreign trade:

Exports—$11 billion: beef, soybeans, cellulose, rice, wheat, wood, dairy products; wool.

Imports—$12.05 billion: refined oil, crude oil, passenger and other transportation vehicles, vehicle parts, cellular phones.

Currency exchange rate: 26.68 Uruguayan pesos = US $1 (2015).

*Gross domestic product (GDP) represents the total value of goods and services produced in a country during a particular year. All figures are 2014 estimates unless otherwise noted.
Source: CIA World Factbook 2015.

country's transportation industry, and some manufacturing firms.

Service industries account for 72 percent of Uruguay's GDP and employ 73 percent of the nation's workforce. Government agencies have the greatest number of service industry workers. Tourism, another leading employer, thrives along Uruguay's Atlantic coast. Many Uruguayans have jobs in hotels, restaurants, and stores at seaside resorts. Others are employed by banks, health care facilities, schools, and firms in the transportation and communication fields.

Industry accounts for 20 percent of Uruguay's GDP and employs 14 percent of all workers. Meat packing and processing is the leading

The port of Montevideo is one of the largest ports in South America.

industry. Other manufactured goods include leather goods, *textiles*, beer, cement, and tires. Most of the nation's industrial plants lie in and around Montevideo.

Agriculture accounts for 7.5 percent of Uruguay's GDP and employs 13 percent of the nation's workers. Livestock raising is the leading source of farm income. Cattle and sheep ranches occupy about four-fifths of Uruguay's total land area. Larger ranches may cover more than 5,000 acres.

Farmers raise crops such as corn, potatoes, sugar beets, sugarcane, and wheat in the fertile soil along the Río Uruguay and the Río de la Plata. Rice is grown in irrigated fields in the east. Most farms have modern mechanical equipment. But the poorest farmers use oxen-drawn plows and old-fashioned methods.

In the 1970s the government, seeing that the fishing industry could generate more revenue, offered aid to fishermen. Currently, a small government-supported fishing fleet catches anchovy, croaker, hake, and weakfish off Uruguay's Atlantic coast. Most of the catch is exported.

Uruguay has few mineral resources. Construction materials, such as gravel, sand, and stone, are the leading mineral products. Uruguay has no deposits of coal, petroleum, or natural gas, and thus must import large quantities of fuel. The country depends almost entirely on hydroelectric power for its electricity. Power plants on the Río Uruguay and the Río Negro supply electricity to all parts of the country.

Uruguay's trading partners include Western European nations, the United States, Mexico, China, Russia, Nigeria, and its neighbors Argentina, Brazil, and Paraguay. These three South American nations, along with Venezuela and Uruguay, are members of a trade federation called MERCO-SUR. Uruguay's major imports include appliances, chemical products, machinery, metal goods, and various fuels. Beef, hides, live cattle and sheep, vegetable products, wool, and woolen textiles rank as the country's leading exports. Uruguay's economic growth is largely due to the high demand for its exports around the world.

TEXT-DEPENDENT QUESTIONS

1. What is Uruguay's most valuable natural resource?
2. What percentage of Uruguayans work in the industrial sector?
3. How is most electricity generated in Uruguay?

(Opposite) A colorfully costumed marcher plays cymbals on the streets of Montevideo during the Uruguayan Carnival celebration in February. (Right) A gaucho rides a wild horse at the El Prado rodeo, which each year draws gauchos from across the country to compete for the "best rider" trophy.

4 A Progressive People and Culture

Uruguay is considered one of the most progressive countries in the world. In 2012, it became the second Latin American country (after Cuba) to allow women to have abortions. In August 2013, Uruguay became the first Latin American country to legally recognize same-sex marriages. Later that year, the government passed laws making it legal to possess and smoke small amounts of marijuana. This made Uruguay one of a handful of countries where marijuana use is legal. Uruguay rates high for most development indicators and is known for its secularism, liberal social laws, and well-developed social security, health, and educational systems.

Makeup of the Population

Almost all of the original Amerindian inhabitants of what is now Uruguay were eventually killed by Spanish settlers or died of diseases brought by the Europeans. Today, there are practically no Amerindians still living in Uruguay.

During the 1800s and early 1900s, large numbers of Spanish and Italian migrant workers moved to Uruguay, joining the descendants of the original Spanish settlers. Most Uruguayans today are descended from these immigrants. Other groups with ancestral ties to Europe include people of English, French, German, and eastern European descent. Though one-quarter of the population claims Italian ancestry, Uruguayans speak Spanish and have built a cultural foundation on Spanish traditions

About 8 percent of Uruguay's people are *mestizos* (people of mixed European and Indian ancestry). About 4 percent are blacks, whose ancestors were brought to Uruguay as slaves during the 1700s and early 1800s. .

Religion

Unlike most other Latin American cultures, Uruguayans never wholly embraced the Roman Catholic Church. The native Indians resisted being Christianized by Catholic missionary priests. In 1837 *civil marriage* was recognized, and in 1861 the state took over public cemeteries. In 1907 divorce

Words to Understand in this Chapter

civil marriage—marriage conducted and recognized by the state.
literacy rate—the percentage of people who can read and write.
middle class—a class of people who are neither rich nor poor.

(which was not recognized by the Catholic Church) was legalized, and in 1909 all religious instruction was banned from state schools. At the urging of President José Batlle y Ordóñez, complete separation of church and state was mandated in the new constitution ratified in 1917. Batlle went so far as to have religious holidays legally renamed.

Today Roman Catholics make up the largest group of Uruguayan believers today, though surveys show that only a small percentage of Uruguayan Catholics attend

The National Shrine of the Sacred Heart of Jesus is a Catholic church that stands on top of a hill in Montevideo.

Mass regularly. Officials of the Catholic Church objected strongly to the same-sex marriage law passed in 2013, but studies show that most Uruguayans support the measure.

During the 20th century, Protestant Christian sects began to grow in importance. From 1960 to 1985, the number of Protestants is estimated to have increased by 60 percent. Today, non-Catholic Christians make up about 11 percent of the population.

Jews make up a small proportion of the population (less than half of 1 percent), with the majority living in Montevideo. The size of the Jewish community has dwindled since 1970, mainly due to emigration.

Social Conditions

Because of the social improvements that swept the country in the early 20th century, Uruguay has a high *literacy rate* and a large urban *middle class*. Income is spread fairly evenly—in other words, wealth is not concentrated in the hands of a small group of people, as is the case in many Latin American countries. The average Uruguayan's standard of living is better than that of most other Latin Americans.

Montevideo, with about 1.3 million inhabitants, is the country's only large city. The rest of the urban population lives in about 20 towns. During the past 20 years, an estimated 500,000 Uruguayans have emigrated, mainly to Argentina and Brazil. Because of Uruguay's low birthrate, high life expectancy, and high percentage of young people who emigrate, Uruguay's population is, on average, older than the populations of most countries.

Family Life

Changes in the law and national custom put Uruguayan women at a far greater advantage than other Latin American women beginning in the late 19th century. Civil, not church, marriage became legally required in 1885, and the influence of the Catholic Church declined. Divorce on the grounds of cruelty by the husband was legalized in 1907. In 1912 women were given the right to divorce if they had a specific cause. Married women were allowed to maintain separate bank accounts as early as 1919. These changes, coupled with access to free public education, opened the door to careers for women in Uruguay. In 1938 they voted for the first time.

Quick Facts: The People of Uruguay

Population: 3,332,972
Ethnic groups: white 88%, mestizo 8%, black 4%, Amerindian (practically nonexistent).
Age structure:
  0–4 years: 21%
  15–64 years: 65.1%
  65 years and over: 13.9%
Population growth rate: 0.26%
Birth rate: 13.18 births/1,000 population
Death rate: 9.48 deaths/1,000 population
Infant mortality rate: 8.97 deaths/1,000 live births
Life expectancy at birth: 76.81 years

Total fertility rate: 1.84 children born/woman
Religions: Roman Catholic 47.1%, non-Catholic Christians 11.1%, nondenominational 23.2%, Jewish 0.3%, atheist or agnostic 17.2%, other 1.1% (2006).
Languages: Spanish (official), Portunol, Brazilero (Portuguese-Spanish mix on the Brazilian frontier).
Literacy (age 15 and older): 98.4% (2012).

All figures are 2014 estimates unless otherwise noted.
Source: CIA World Factbook 2014.

By 1960 one-quarter of all Uruguayan women were in the workforce, finding help at home from the large number of housekeepers willing to cook, clean, and take care of children for modest wages. By 1975 one-fifth of all Uruguayan households were headed by women. Now, close to 60 percent of women work outside their home.

Middle-class Uruguayan families tend to be small—about 3.5 persons per household. Most women practice birth control. In rural areas, however, families tend to be larger and more unstable. Common-law marriages (unions with no legal contract) are widespread, as are instances of babies born out of wedlock.

Uruguay's educational system is excellent. Teaching is a respected

Members of Uruguay's national team celebrate a victory. The team has won the South American championship 15 times, more than any other nation.

profession and pays well. It is expected that girls will go to school and have careers. However, the schools in rural areas usually lack supplies, good classrooms, and better teachers.

Family gatherings in Uruguay often center on outdoor barbecues (*asados*). Another typical custom, symbolic of family and friendship ties, is the sharing of yerba maté, a form of green tea. A hollowed-out gourd (the maté), or sometimes a china cup, is packed almost full with green tea leaves. A metal straw is inserted into the tea, and boiling water is poured on top. The maté is then passed around in a circle, each person adding a little more hot water. Uruguayans drink gallons of maté every week.

Asados, parades, and other public celebrations often include folk music and dancing. Most of the country's musical and dance traditions (folk songs, polkas, waltzes) emerged from Europe, with the exception of the *candombe*, an African-influenced dance dating from colonial times.

Sports and recreation offer other occasions to bring families together. Amateur and professional soccer (called *fútbol* in Spanish) is very popular among the middle and lower classes. People of the upper classes generally prefer tennis, golf, and sailing. They usually try to escape Montevideo for the beach resorts on weekends and during the long summer holidays of December and January. For the rich, membership in a country club is a symbol of social status.

Meat, the Main Dish

Uruguayans are avid meat-eaters and the *parrillada* (beef platter) is popular everywhere. The majority of Uruguayan restaurants are beef grill-rooms, which specialize in the country's most famous traditional dish, *asado* (barbecued beef).

Beef is eaten in most meals and comes in many forms, including *asado de tira* (ribs), *pulpa* (boneless beef), *lomo* (fillet steak), and *bife de chorizo* (rump steak). *Costillas* (chops) and *milanesa* (a veal cutlet), also popular, are usually eaten with mixed salad or chips. *Chivito* is a sandwich filled with slices of meat, lettuce, and egg. Other local dishes are *puchero* (beef with vegetables, bacon, beans, and sausages); pizza; barbecued pork; grilled chicken in wine; *cazuela* (stew), which is usually served with *mondongo* (tripe); seafood; *morcilla dulce* (sweet black sausage made from blood, orange peel, and walnuts); and *morcilla salada* (salty sausage).

TEXT-DEPENDENT QUESTIONS

1. What percentage of Uruguay's population is mestizo?
2. How many Uruguayans adhere to the Roman Catholic religion?
3. What beverage is shared as a symbol of family and friendship ties?

Two views of Montevideo, the capital of Uruguay and the country's most important city. (Opposite) An aerial view of the harbor and downtown skyline as seen from the Spanish colonial fortress atop El Cerro. (Right) Colorfully painted houses in one of the city's neighborhoods.

5 Cities and Towns of Uruguay

NEARLY HALF OF Uruguay's 3.3 million people live in or near the capital city, Montevideo. What Uruguayans consider to be the other cities in the country are really large towns. This settlement pattern is unprecedented in history, except in the city-states of the ancient world, where the city was the nation. The reason Uruguay's population is so concentrated is that the country's vast pastureland is too valuable to the economy to develop.

How People Live

Most of the people in Montevideo and other Uruguayan cities belong to the country's large middle class. Many middle-class city dwellers hold government or professional jobs or work in business and industry. They live in apartments or in comfortable single-family houses. Business executives, government leaders, and other well-to-do city dwellers live in luxurious high-rise apartment buildings or mansions.

Uruguay's urban population also includes factory workers, unskilled laborers, household servants, and other people with low-paying jobs. A small number of these working-class people live in tiny shacks on the cities' outskirts. But Uruguay has fewer urban slums than do most other Latin American countries. Electricity, running water, and sewers are available to all but the poorest city dwellers.

Many of the people who live in Uruguay's rural areas own or rent small farms. Many of them live in one-story *adobe* houses. Others work as wage laborers on large plantations or as gauchos on huge ranches called *estancias*. Shacks with thatch roofs and mud floors serve as housing for families of migrant laborers and ranch workers. Many wealthy landowners have homes in the cities in addition to their country estates.

In general, rural Uruguayans have a lower standard of living than do urban Uruguayans. As a result, many rural people move to the cities in search of a better life.

Montevideo

Montevideo was founded in 1726 on a high hill beside a large bay that forms a perfect natural harbor. Its strategic location on the Río de la Plata,

Words to Understand in this Chapter

adobe—a brick or building material of sun-dried earth and straw.
estancia—a ranch.

below the Portuguese settlement of Colônia do Sacramento, helped counter Portuguese expansion from Brazil. But Montevideo grew into a commercial center as well, thanks to its port. In the 19th century, the British promoted Montevideo as a rival port to Buenos Aires.

The city has expanded to such an extent that today its covers most of its department (a regional division similar to a county in the United States).The original area of settlement, known as the Old City, lies next to the port. But the central business district and the middle-class residential areas have moved eastward. The only exception is that banking and finance businesses

The Plaza Independencia, Montevideo, features the Palacio Salvo. At the time of its completion in 1928, the neo-Gothic structure was South America's tallest building, at 275 feet (84 meters).

continue to cluster in the Old City around the Stock Exchange, the Bank of Uruguay, and the Central Bank of Uruguay.

Today, Greater Montevideo is by far the most developed region of Uruguay and surpasses other regions economically and culturally. It is home to the country's two universities, its principal hospitals, and most of its communications media—television stations, radio stations, newspapers, and magazines.

Until a construction boom during the late 1970s, there were few modern buildings in Montevideo. In many parts of the city, elegant 19th-century houses built around a central patio are still commonplace. Some have large open-air patios. But most are covered by a glass roof that is sometimes made of colorful stained glass. Few of these houses are still owned by single families, however. Many have been turned into low-cost apartments.

The middle class of Montevideo tends to live in more modern apartments near the city center or the University of the Republic. Some choose a single-family *villa* with a small backyard. Many of these are close to the beaches running east from the downtown area along the avenue known as La Rambla, Montevideo's most important thoroughfare.

A beautiful metropolis, Montevideo offers extensive cultural activities and sightseeing opportunities. Attractions include the neoclassical Teatro Solís, which was completed in 1856 and named for the ill-fated Spanish explorer killed by natives in 1516.

The Plaza Independencia, a large square situated in the heart of the modern city, is lined by palm trees and dominated by a statue of José Gervasio Artigas, who is buried in the plaza. The neo-Gothic Palacio Salvo stands on

Quick Facts: Uruguay's 10 Largest Cities

		Population				Population
1	Montevideo	1,319,108	6	Rivera		64,465
2	Salto	104,028	7	Maldonado		62,590
3	Ciudad de la Costa	95,176	8	Tacuarembó		54,755
4	Paysandú	76,412	9	Melo		51,830
5	Las Piedras	71,258	10	Mercedes		41,974

Figures from the 2011 census. Source: Source: Instituto Nacional de Estadística, Uruguay.

the edge of the Plaza Independencia and marks the start of the Avenida 18 de Julio, Montevideo's premier shopping locale. Avenida 18 de Julio boasts a myriad of boutiques featuring the latest fashions and fine wool garments for all seasons.

Rimming the Plaza Constitución, Montevideo's oldest square, are two historic buildings: the Cabildo (old town hall) and the Catedral Metropolitana (Metropolitan Cathedral). The ornate cathedral was completed in 1790.

The magnificent Palacio Legislativo took more than two decades to build; it has housed Uruguay's national legislature, the General Assembly, since 1925. The upper house, the Chamber of Senators, has 30 seats; the lower house, the Chamber of Representatives, has 99 seats. All legislators are elected to five-year terms by popular vote.

Among Montevideo's other attractions are many historic buildings,

Small boats in the harbor at Punta del Este, a fashionable resort on the coast.

along with parks, plazas, and statuary. The city is also known as a good place to shop. Ceramic and leather goods are specialties.

Punta del Este

About an hour's drive east of Montevideo, in the coastal area of the country nicknamed "the Uruguayan Riviera," lies the fashionable resort town of Punta del Este. One of the most popular vacation destinations in all of southern South America, the town attracts many well-to-do Brazilians, Argentines, and Uruguayans to its lovely beaches. Because it is located on a narrow peninsula, Punta del Este had to build up, and today it is blanketed by high-rise hotels, apartments, and condominiums that fill during the summer months with sun-loving travelers.

Other Towns and Cities

In addition to Punta del Este, the Uruguayan Riviera boasts dozens of beach resorts for vacationers. The old city of Maldonado, with its historic buildings, is also popular.

Salto (or Embalse de Salto Grande), founded about 1817, lies in northwestern Uruguay on the Río Uruguay, opposite the town of Concordia, Argentina. It is the second-largest city in the country and a road and rail hub. With a surrounding region that produces livestock, citrus fruit, sugarcane, grapes, and honey, Salto is a center for trade in grains and vegetables and also has a school of agriculture. Industries there include flour milling, meatpacking, shipbuilding, and the manufacture of chemicals, drugs, and wickerwork. Nearby are Salto Grande (the river falls) and the resort town of Arenitas Blancas.

Paysandú in western Uruguay is also located on the Río Uruguay. Founded in 1772, the city is a busy river port for oceangoing ships and has meatpacking plants, tanneries, and flour mills.

Las Piedras in southern Uruguay is near Montevideo. It is a rail and commercial center for a wine-growing and agricultural region. The gaucho nationalist leader José Gervasio Artigas scored a victory for Uruguayan independence over the Spanish here in 1811.

Rivera, in northern Uruguay, lies opposite the Brazilian city of Santana do Livramento, with which it shares a central street. The northernmost stopping point of the Uruguayan railroad system, Rivera is in an area producing fruits, livestock, tobacco, cotton, grains, and vegetables. It is also a cattle and sheep market. Textiles and tobacco products are manufactured in Rivera as well.

Melo, in northeastern Uruguay near the Brazil border, is an important regional transportation, manufacturing, and commercial center. The Spanish founded Melo in 1795 as a military post.

Mercedes, located in southwestern Uruguay, lies beside the Río Negro, near its mouth on the Río Uruguay. The city, which has road, rail, and air links to the capital, is a river port and trade center for the cattle, sheep, grains, and flax that are raised in the area. Industries include a prized wool market, grain processing, linseed-oil milling, and paper milling. A yachting center and health resort, the city also has a well-known musical society, an extensive rose garden, and parks along the river.

Festivals and Fiestas

Uruguay's most famous festival is the annual Carnival, which takes place on the Monday and Tuesday immediately preceding Ash Wednesday, the start of the Christian season of Lent. (Carnival may fall in February or March.) Most shops and businesses close for the entire week. Houses and streets are decorated, and comedy shows are staged at open-air theaters.

During the colonial period, black slaves used to perform their ancestral African dances and songs next to the fortified walls of Montevideo. White masters and their families would watch from the top of the walls on Sunday afternoons. When slavery was abolished, black Uruguayans continued their traditions, which, as time passed, maintained black folklore, the *candombe* and the distinctive drum rhythms accompanying it, and the carnival processions of performing groups. Las Llamadas, a special evening celebration carried out during Carnival, attracts thousands of tourists and local citizens. Dozens of bands representing different parts of Montevideo get together and perform. Local residents can tell where the musicians come from by the way they play.

In most Latin American countries, Holy Week—the week leading up to Easter Sunday—is a time of large public ceremonies linked to the Catholic faith. Because Uruguay maintains separation of church and state, however, Holy Week observances are generally confined to the insides of churches. In fact, coinciding with Holy Week each year are two secular (nonreligious) festivals: Tourism Week and La Semana Criolla (Creole Week), a popular celebration where the most outstanding riders in Uruguay and the neighboring countries come to show their skill. Spectators thrill to see bronco and bull riding, lasso tricks, and horse races.

Throughout the year, the Port Marquet neighborhood of Montevideo is a popular place to visit. This marketplace, constructed in the 19th century, is today a cheerful collection of barbecue restaurants. The streets are outdoor performance areas for musicians, jugglers, drummers, and watercolor artists.

Outside of Montevideo, old *estancias* (ranches) feature country food and folk shows throughout the year. In the towns, shops offer typical souvenirs such as *bombillas* (small tubes for drinking maté), *boleadoras* (hunting weapons used by gauchos), whips, harnesses, and saddles, as well as a variety of leather and wood crafts.

TEXT-DEPENDENT QUESTIONS

1. When was Montevideo founded?
2. What two historic buildings are located near the Plaza Constitución?
3. What important river port in in western Uruguay was founded in 1772?

Unlike most Latin American countries, Uruguay maintains a separation of church and state, both constitutionally and by tradition. This is reflected in the country's fiestas and festivals. Whereas important Roman Catholic feast days are occasions for public holidays or large festivals in other Latin American nations, in Uruguay this is generally not the case.

January

January 1, **New Year's Day**, is celebrated throughout Uruguay.

Uruguayans mark January 6, which in other Spanish-speaking Latin American countries is the religious holiday of Three Kings Day or Epiphany, as **Children's Day**. It is an occasion for gift-giving.

Also on January 6 is an important annual horse race similar in some respects to America's Kentucky Derby: the **José Pedro Ramírez Grand Horse Race**. Held at the Maroñas Racetrack, it attracts fans from all over Uruguay as well as Argentina and Brazil.

February

During **Carnival**, a two-day celebration preceding Ash Wednesday, Uruguayans hold parties and have parades featuring colorfully dressed marchers and musicians. (Carnival may also occur in March, depending when Easter falls in the given year.) **Las Llamadas**, a Carnival activity held at night, features performances by dozens of bands from throughout Montevideo; it attracts tens of thousands of tourists and locals.

March

Coinciding with **Semana Santa** (Holy Week) in Uruguay are the festivals of **Tourism Week** and **Creole Week**. The former features barbecues and folk music. The latter focuses on bronco and bull riding, horse races, and gaucho skills competitions.

Uruguay's Christians do celebrate **Easter** (which may fall in April in some years) by attending Mass and eating a large meal with family, but it is primarily a private matter, unlike Easter in other Latin American nations.

May

May 1 in Uruguay is celebrated as **Día de los Trabajadores** (Workers Day).

The **Battle of Las Piedras**, a victory by José Gervasio Artigas, is commemorated on the sixth of the month.

June

June 19, the **Birthday of José Artigas**, is a national holiday.

July

Constitution Day is celebrated throughout Uruguay on July 18.

August

August 25 is **Independence Day**, marking the date in 1825 when Uruguayan rebels declared their freedom from Brazil.

October

October 12, **Columbus Day** or **Día de la Raza**, is a national holiday.

The 12th is also the day Uruguayans remember the important **Battle of Sarandí**.

November

On November 2, Uruguayans remember the dead. This is the **Día de los Muertos** (All Souls' Day).

December

The 25th of the month is **Christmas**, which Uruguayans typically celebrate with their families. In Uruguay the day is also called **Family Day**, a further reminder of the government's efforts to remove religion from public life.

 **Recipes**

Celery and Pea Soup *(Sopa de Apio y Guisantes)*

(Serves 6)
1 head celery, chopped
6 cups vegetable stock
1 bay leaf
1 clove
6 tbsp corn oil
1 onion, chopped
1 clove garlic, chopped
6 carrots, scraped and chopped
1 tbsp all-purpose flour
1 lb tomatoes, peeled, seeded, and chopped
6 lbs young peas, defrosted, if frozen
Salt, freshly ground pepper

Directions:
1. Put celery into a large saucepan with the stock, bay leaf, and clove, bring to a simmer, cover, and simmer for 10 minutes. Set aside.
2. Remove the bay leaf and clove.
3. In a frying pan heat the oil and sauté the onion, garlic, bacon, and carrot until the vegetables are soft. Stir in the flour and cook for 1–2 minutes.
4. Add the tomatoes, stir and cook for 5 minutes.
5. Add all the cooked ingredients to the stock with the celery, cover and simmer for 5 minutes.
6. Remove the solids, place in a food processor, and reduce to a purée, then push through a sieve set over the saucepan.
7. Season to taste with salt and pepper. Cook the peas and simmer until they are tender, about 10 minutes.

Ambrosia

(Serves 4)
5 egg yolks
2 cups milk
1 tbsp cloves
Half a lemon, grated
1 cup sugar
1/2 cup water
1 tbsp vanilla

Directions:
1. Lightly beat 5 egg yolks and mix them with 2 cups of milk. Add gratings of lemon and cloves.
2. In another saucepan make a syrup with the sugar and water. Heat the water in a saucepan and mix in the sugar, stirring constantly until golden. Cool slightly.
3. Remove the syrup from the heat and pour into the mix of eggs and milk.
4. Put the mixture over the heat and cook it, stirring until clots appear and the liquid is concentrated.
5. Add vanilla and serve cold in bowls or cups.

Pascualina Pie

(Serves 8)
1 lb beets or spinach
1 onion, chopped
1 clove garlic, chopped
Pinch of grated nutmeg
Pinch of pepper
4 tbsp oil
3 tbsp grated Parmesan cheese
6 eggs
2 rounds of premade pie crust

Directions:
1. Preheat oven to 325°F.
2. Boil the spinach (or the beets, or a mix of both). Once cooked, drain well to remove all water. Mash the vegetables.
3. Brown the onion and garlic in the oil in a frying pan, and add the vegetables. Season with pepper and nutmeg. Set aside when the mixture is hot.
4. Cover the bottom of a pie dish with one round of pie crust. Pour the vegetables into the pie crust. Make five shallow holes in the vegetables to place the eggs (raw), like five points of a star, an inch or so away from the edge of the dish. Sprinkle Parmesan cheese over the top.
5. Cover the whole with the second pie crust and close, sealing firmly the edges.
6. Bake at 325° F as long as necessary for the crust to turn brown and flaky. When cut into slices, each piece will show the white and yellow of the eggs inside.

Stewed Lentils

(Serves 8)
1 lb lentils
6 cups water
3 medium carrots, sliced
1 onion, chopped
1 red pepper, chopped
1 tbsp (or cube) powdered vegetable broth
1 tbsp vinegar
Salt and pepper

Directions:
1. Sort the lentils and wash them.
2. Soak the lentils for 4–5 hours.
3. In a pot big enough to easily hold six cups of water, brown the onion and the sweet pepper.
4. Add the water, lentils, carrots, and powdered vegetable broth. Simmer covered for about two hours.
5. Once the lentils are tender, add the vinegar.

Amerindian—a term for the indigenous peoples of North, Central, and South America before the arrival of Europeans in the late 15th century.

Carnival—a popular festival in many South American countries, characterized by parades, dancing, and ornate costumes. It is celebrated just before the start of the Roman Catholic season of Lent, the 40-day period before Easter Sunday.

civil liberty—the right of people to do or say things that are not illegal without being stopped or interrupted by the government.

Communism—a political system in which all resources, industries, and property are considered to be held in common by all the people, with government as the central authority responsible for controlling all economic and social activity.

coup d'état—the violent overthrow of an existing government by a small group.

criollo—a resident of Spain's New World colonies who was born in North America to parents of Spanish ancestry. During the colonial period, criollos ranked above mestizos in the social order.

deforestation—the action or process of clearing forests.

economic system—the production, distribution, and consumption of goods and services within a country.

embargo—a government restriction or restraint on commerce, especially an order that prohibits trade with a particular nation.

foreign aid—financial assistance given by one country to another.

free trade—trade based on the unrestricted exchange of goods, with tariffs (taxes) only used to create revenue, not keep out foreign goods.

indigenous people—a name for native Amerindian tribes that lived in an area before Europeans came to settle there.

Latin America—a term for the areas of the American continents in which Spanish or Portuguese are the main languages. It includes nearly all of the Americas, except Canada, the United States, and a few small countries like Suriname and Guyana.

mestizo—a person of mixed Amerindian and European (typically Spanish) descent.

plaza—the central open square at the center of colonial-era cities in Latin America.

plebiscite—a vote by which the people of an entire country express their opinion on a particular government or national policy.

population density—a measurement of the number of people living in a specific area, such a square mile or square kilometer.

pre-Columbian—referring to a time before the 1490s, when Christopher Columbus landed in the Americas.

regime—a period of rule by a particular government, especially one that is considered to be oppressive.

Roman Catholicism—a Christian religion in which adherents obey the dictates of the Pope, whose headquarters is the Vatican in Rome. Roman Catholicism is the world's largest Christian denomination, with more than 1.2 billion members worldwide. Nearly 40 percent of Catholics live in Latin America.

service industry—any business, organization, or profession that does work for a customer, but is not involved in manufacturing.

Travel Posters

Make a colorful travel poster advertising Uruguay as a place to visit. Use printed pictures from Internet travel sites to illustrate the poster.

Comparison Bar Graph

Create a bar graph showing the populations of the 10 largest cities in Uruguay and the 10 largest in the United States. Use two colors.

Exchange Student

Pretend that you were an exchange student in Uruguay last year, and make a scrapbook of your experience.

- Present to the class a picture of the flag (in color) from the country.
- Try to find an example of Uruguayan currency (major airport currency exchanges and some banks carry it). Find out what the exchange rate is between our country and Uruguay.
- Prepare a map and point out the city where you "lived." Be sure to pronounce the Spanish name correctly.
- Show some of the historic or popular places on the map that you visited with your imagined family. Why are they famous? Supply pictures.
- Play some music recordings from Uruguay.

Questions to Answer in a Paragraph

- What are the uses of a reservoir like Lake Rincón del Bonete in Uruguay?
- What are wetlands? (See Chapter 1.) Why are they important?
- Who were the Tupamaros? What did they demand?
- How is leather made?
- Who are gauchos?
- What happened to the Charrúa Indians?

Class Game

Divide the class in half. Have a contest to see who can spell the glossary words correctly, and then who can give correct definitions for each word. Finally, break into smaller teams and see which team can correctly use the greatest number of glossary words in a single sentence.

Chronology

1516	Charrúa Indians kill a party of Spanish soldiers led by explorer Juan Díaz de Solís. Their hostility discourages Spanish settlement.
1603	Spanish colonists release cattle and horses on the open plains of what is now Uruguay, then known as the Banda Oriental. The livestock thrive in the mild climate.
1680–83	The Portuguese and the Spanish compete to control trade in the Plata estuary.
1726	Montevideo, the future capital of Uruguay, is founded.
1811	José Gervasio Artigas leads soldiers to initiate a revolt against the Spanish forces vying for control of Montevideo and the rest of the Banda Oriental.
1828	Inspired by the brave revolts led by José Gervasio Artigas, Juan Antonio Lavalleja and his team of patriots, called the 33 Immortals, liberate the Banda Oriental from Brazil.
1865–70	Uruguay unites with Brazil and Argentina to fight against Paraguay in the War of the Triple Alliance.
1885	Civil marriages become legally required, replacing church marriages and further reducing the influence of the Roman Catholic Church.
Late 1800s–Early 1900s	Large numbers of Spanish and Italian migrant workers immigrate to Uruguay.
1903–7, 1911–15	President José Batlle y Ordóñez launches social programs that include medical-aid and retirement plans, free education, laws protecting workers' rights, and public health reforms. The middle class expands and Uruguay gains a reputation for social harmony.
1920	Uruguay joins the League of Nations.
1931	Blanco Party elects Gabriel Terra, who demands stronger governmental control.

1938	Colorado Party returns to power; a renewed constitution strengthens individual liberties.
1967	The Tupamaros, an urban guerrilla movement, use violence to demand reforms.
1971	The military, citing the threat posed by the Tupamaros, takes control of the Uruguayan government and initiates a harsh crackdown on guerrillas and government critics.
1984	Julio María Sanguinetti is elected president, ending a long period of authoritarian rule.
2001	Hoof-and-mouth disease in Uruguay's cattle damages the beef industry; economic and political problems in Brazil and Argentina begin to harm Uruguay's economy.
2002	Economic upheaval continues with rising unemployment and decreased GDP; the government temporarily suspends banking activity as an emergency measure, leading to riots.
2004	Tabaré Vásquez Rosas, a doctor and Montevideo's former mayor, is elected president.
2005	Vásquez re-establishes Uruguay's diplomatic relations with Cuba.
2007	A paper mill is constructed along the Uruguay River, angering environmentalists; Uruguay approves same-sex civil unions.
2010	Mercosur member-states, including Uruguay, sign a free-trade agreement with Israel.
2013	Uruguay legalises both same-sex marriage and the cultivation and consumption of marijuana for recreational use.
2014	In November, voters return Tabaré Vásquez to the presidency.

Further Reading / Internet Resources

Burford, Tim. *Uruguay*. Chalfont St Peter, UK: Bradt Travel Guides, 2014.

Chasteen, John Charles. *Born in Blood and Fire: A Concise History of Latin America*. New York: W.W. Norton, 2011.

Morrison, Marion. *Uruguay*. New York: Children's Press, 2005.

Espater, Anna Maria. *Uruguay*. Bath, UK: Footprint, 2014.

Williamson, Edwin. *The Penguin History of Latin America*. New York: Penguin Group, 2010.

Travel Information

http://www.worldtravelguide.net/uruguay
http://www.lonelyplanet.com/uruguay

History and Geography

http://www.encyclopedia.com/doc/1G2-2586700177.html#HISTORY
http://www.iexplore.com/dmap/Uruguay/History

Economic and Political Information

http://www.state.gov/r/pa/ei/bgn/2091.htm
https://www.cia.gov/llibrary/publications/the-world-factbook/geos/uy.html

Caribbean/Latin American Action
1625 K Street NW, Suite 200
Washington, DC 20006
Phone: (202) 464-2031
Website: www.c-caa.org

The Embassy of Uruguay
1913 Eye Street, NW
Washington, D.C. 20006
(202) 331-1313
(202) 331-8142
Website: www.uruwashi.org
Email: uruwashi@uruwashi.org

U.S. Agency for International Development
Ronald Reagan Building
Washington, D.C. 20523-0001
Phone: (202) 712-0000
Website: www.usaid.gov
Email: pinquiries@usaid.gov

U.S. Department of Commerce
International Trade Administration
Office of Latin America and the Caribbean
1401 Constitution Ave., NW
Washington, D.C. 20230
Phone: (202) 482-2000
Fax: (202) 482-5168
Website: www.commerce.gov
Email: publicaffairs@doc.gov

Index

Contributors

Senior Consulting Editor **James D. Henderson** is professor of international studies at Coastal Carolina University. He is the author of *Conservative Thought in Twentieth Century Latin America: The Ideals of Laureano Gómez* (1988; Spanish edition *Las ideas de Laureano Gómez* published in 1985); *When Colombia Bled: A History of the Violence in Tolima* (1985; Spanish edition *Cuando Colombia se desangró, una historia de la Violencia en metrópoli y provincia*, 1984); and coauthor of *A Reference Guide to Latin American History* (2000) and *Ten Notable Women of Latin America* (1978).

Mr. Henderson earned a bachelor's degree in history from Centenary College of Louisiana, and a master's degree in history from the University of Arizona. He then spent three years in the Peace Corps, serving in Colombia, before earning his doctorate in Latin American history in 1972 at Texas Christian University.

Charles J. Shields is the author of 30 books for young people. He has degrees in English and history from the University of Illinois, Urbana-Champaign. Before turning to writing full-time, he was chairman of the English and guidance departments at Homewood-Flossmoor High School in Flossmoor, Illinois. He lives in Homewood, a suburb of Chicago, with his wife, Guadalupe, a former elementary school principal and now an educational consultant to the Chicago Public Schools.